2 Timothy

30-DAY DEVOTIONAL

2 Timothy

Michael Baughen
with Elizabeth McQuoid

FOOD
FOR THE
JOURNEY

INTER-VARSITY PRESS
36 Causton Street, London SW1P 4ST, England
Email: ivp@ivpbooks.com
Website: www.ivpbooks.com

First published 2016

British Library Cataloguing-in-Publication Data
A catalogue record for this book is available from the British Library.

ISBN: 978–1–78359–438–2
eBook ISBN: 978–1–78359–444–3

Typeset in Great Britain by CRB Associates, Potterhanworth, Lincolnshire
Printed in Great Britain by Ashford Colour Press Ltd, Gosport, Hampshire

Inter-Varsity Press publishes Christian books that are true to the Bible and that communicate the gospel, develop discipleship and strengthen the church for its mission in the world.

IVP originated within the Inter-Varsity Fellowship, now the Universities and Colleges Christian Fellowship, a student movement connecting Christian Unions in universities and colleges throughout Great Britain, and a member movement of the International Fellowship of Evangelical Students. Website: www.uccf.org.uk. That historic association is maintained, and all senior IVP staff and committee members subscribe to the UCCF Basis of Faith.

Preface

Can you guess how many sermons have been preached from the Keswick platform? Almost 6,500!

For over 140 years, the Keswick Convention in the English Lake District has welcomed gifted expositors from all over the world. The convention's archive is a treasure trove of sermons preached on every book of the Bible.

This series is an invitation to mine that treasure. It takes talks from the Bible Reading series given by well-loved Keswick speakers, past and present, and reformats them into daily devotionals. Where necessary, the language has been updated but, on the whole, it is the message you would have heard had you been listening in the tent on Skiddaw Street. Each day of the devotional ends with a newly written section designed to help you apply God's Word to your own life and situation.

Whether you are a convention regular or have never been to Keswick, this Food for the Journey series provides a unique opportunity to study the Scriptures with a Bible teacher by your side. Each book is designed to fit in your jacket pocket or handbag so you can read it anywhere – over the breakfast table, on the commute into work or college, while you are waiting in your car, during your lunch break or in bed at night. Wherever life's journey takes you, time in God's Word is vital nourishment for your spiritual journey.

Our prayer is that these devotionals become your daily feast, a precious opportunity to meet with God through his Word. Read, meditate, apply and pray through the Scriptures given for each day, and allow God's truths to take root and transform your life.

If these devotionals whet your appetite for more, there is a 'For further study' section at the end of each book. You can also visit our website at www.keswickministries.org/resources to find the full range of books, study guides, CDs, DVDs and mp3s available. Why not order an audio recording of the Bible Reading series to accompany your daily devotional?

Let the word of Christ dwell in you richly.
(Colossians 3:16, ESV)

Introduction
2 Timothy

Last words.

Last words are important. They are a brief glimpse into another person's soul. A final unveiling of what mattered most.

The second letter of Timothy records Paul's last words. He is in prison, near to death, dictating this letter to Luke for his young pastor friend Timothy. As he sits chained to a Roman soldier, Paul's passion for the gospel shines out. He uses his farewell message to urge Timothy to maintain his focus on the fundamentals of the faith. There will be distractions, opposition, and even suffering, but Timothy is to keep Christ and the gospel central to his life and ministry. Paul charges Timothy, and the church in every subsequent generation, to share this gospel faithfully and urgently.

This intensely personal letter invites us into Paul's prison cell, allows us to hear his last words, and gives us an insight into his devotion to God. It challenges us to think about our own legacy. What are we living for? Or rather, whom are we living for?

Day 1

Read 2 Timothy 1:1–18
Key verses: 2 Timothy 1:1–2

....

> [1] *Paul, an apostle of Christ Jesus by the will of God, in keeping with the promise of life that is in Christ Jesus,*
>
> [2] *To Timothy, my dear son:*
>
> *Grace, mercy and peace from God the Father and Christ Jesus our Lord.*

All of us are called to serve Christ. That service may be in your home, your workplace, university campus or in church. God has put you there, he has called you there, and you serve him there, 'by the will of God'.

Paul knows he is an apostle 'by the will of God'. He is in prison. He will never again be able to pioneer new churches. There will be no more missionary journeys. He is about to die for his faith. But Paul is still convinced that he is what he is, and where he is, 'by the will of God'. It's a phrase that should burn into us. When difficulties come, cling on to this truth like a rock in a storm. It may be that like Paul you are no longer able to do many of the things you did in the past; but still see that what you are and where you are is 'by the will of God'.

As an apostle, Paul's goal was to preach the good news; to share the 'promise of life that is in Christ Jesus'. This letter is Paul's charge to Timothy, a young pastor in Ephesus, and to us, to pass on to the next generation all that the apostles witnessed. He wants us to guard, follow and share the truth about Jesus with others.

Paul's role as an apostle was unique. But each of us, in our own situations, are called to share the life of Christ with others. Wherever you are, 'by the will of God', whatever your daily circumstances are, look for opportunities to speak and live out the good news of Jesus. And do so confident of God's:

- *grace*: all the wonder of being in Christ, of full and free salvation and of undeserved love

- *mercy*: the withholding of the punishment our sin deserved

- *peace*: the wholeness of mind, body, spirit and soul as Christ makes us fully his.

Consider for a moment your job, your family responsibilities, your church ministry – all the different strands that make up your life. It might not be the scenario you'd imagined or hoped for, but God has placed you there. And his greatest delight is to see Christ's life shine out as, with the Holy Spirit's help, you daily choose to live for him. Amazingly, like the cracked clay jars in 2 Corinthians 4:7, God uses our ordinary and often broken lives to display Christ's life to others. Today as you meditate on God's grace, mercy and peace, thank him for where he has placed you. Look for ways to share the promise of life that is in Christ.

Day 2

Read 2 Timothy 1:3–18

Key verses: 2 Timothy 1:3–5

....

³I thank God, whom I serve, as my ancestors did, with a clear conscience, as night and day I constantly remember you in my prayers. ⁴Recalling your tears, I long to see you, so that I may be filled with joy. ⁵I am reminded of your sincere faith, which first lived in your grandmother Lois and in your mother Eunice and, I am persuaded, now lives in you also.

A little bit of encouragement goes a long way! Everyone needs encouragement; it's how we're wired. Your interest in someone else's life could have a profound impact, without you even realizing it.

Paul was deeply concerned for Timothy. Timothy was not an extrovert or a strong personality. He didn't find it easy to be a Christian leader, particularly when the going was rough. He had a natural tendency that we're all familiar with, to duck out of problems, suffering or controversy.

And Paul wants to strengthen him. So, in verses 3 and 4, he reminds Timothy that he is deeply concerned for him.

Each of us needs to demonstrate concern for others. We can show concern for young people going off to college. It only takes a moment to pray, to write, to show you care. How Timothy's heart must have thumped in his throat as he read Paul's letter: 'I thank God, Timothy, as I remember you.' Paul remembering and thanking God for me! Believing that God is working in me! Paul, this giant in Timothy's eyes, is actually somebody who thanks God for him. He is on Paul's prayer list!

Who is on your prayer list? Whom are you encouraging or concerned for? Church is full of people needing encouragement, such as parents with special needs children, those with older children and an 'empty nest', young people facing the pressure to conform in secondary school, older folk feeling the burden of advancing years. The list is endless!

Praying for someone is more than sentimental encouragement. It is more than a reminder of the deep desire that we should run well for Christ – although it is all of these things; it is a means of the grace of God in answer to prayer. Timothy will be strengthened by the reminder that Paul's heart aches for him in the bonds of deep love, and is expectant of his service for Christ.

Life is busy. It's easy for every day to be filled with our immediate needs and responsibilities, with little or no time left to remember others. But think back to those mature Christians who encouraged you. What difference did their prayers make? Whom could you be praying for? How could you encourage a younger person? Just think – your prayers could be the means of God's grace in someone else's life.

Day 3

Read 2 Timothy 1:3–18
Key verses: 2 Timothy 1:6–7

....

⁶For this reason I remind you to fan into flame the gift of God, which is in you through the laying on of my hands. ⁷For the Spirit God gave us does not make us timid, but gives us power, love and self-discipline.

Do you know what your spiritual gift is? Paul tells us each of us has a gift (1 Corinthians 7:7), but many of us are not sure how to discover it or what to do if we find it!

Here Paul reminds Timothy that God has called him to ministry and equipped him for it. He encourages Timothy to think back to when his gift was received through the laying on of hands. This laying on of hands is normally a sign of prayer to God in response to a person's commitment. So the church responded to Timothy's commitment to the task by the laying on of hands. Together they asked God to equip him for the task to which he had called him.

The important point is that Timothy didn't sit around doing nothing, waiting for God to send him the right gifts. God sends the right gifts when we respond to the right task.

Imagine God's spiritual gifts as being like the flames of a fire. You have to keep fanning the flames and fuelling the fire to keep it fully alive. How do you keep your spiritual gift alive? By reflection, prayer, devotion, using the gift and proving God's grace, and training to be a better user of the gift. Don't try to serve God without using his gifts. It's pointless, careless and fatal for effective ministry.

So Paul urges Timothy that whatever the opposition, the materialism of society, his own immaturity, ill health or shyness, he is Christ's man. He is called by him, equipped by him, and he must keep that equipment fresh.

Like Timothy, God has equipped us for serving him with spiritual gifts and the indwelling of the Holy Spirit. God's Spirit in us means we can serve, not in fear, but with:

- *power*: that enables us, gives us boldness, helps us endure, and means we can triumph even in weakness

- *love*: self-giving love that thinks of others and does not count the cost

- *self-discipline*: attitudes and behaviour that seek God's glory, not our own.

What task has God given you? There are many jobs in church life, like putting the chairs out, which just have to be done. But there are other tasks that you have been uniquely designed and equipped for. These tasks often change through the various seasons of life. Ask God to show you what he wants you to do for him now. Pray he will equip you for the task, whether it's parenting, preaching or catering. Be conscious of serving God today in his power, with love and with self-discipline.

Day 4

Read 2 Timothy 1:3–18
Key verses: 2 Timothy 1:8–12a

. . . .

⁸So do not be ashamed of the testimony about our Lord or of me his prisoner. Rather, join with me in suffering for the gospel, by the power of God. ⁹He has saved us and called us to a holy life – not because of anything we have done but because of his own purpose and grace. This grace was given us in Christ Jesus before the beginning of time, ¹⁰but it has now been revealed through the appearing of our Saviour, Christ Jesus, who has destroyed death and has brought life and immortality to light through the gospel. ¹¹And of this gospel I was appointed a herald and an apostle and a teacher. ¹²That is why I am suffering as I am.

Do you believe the gospel? Do you believe it enough to work for it, share it, and accept the inevitable suffering that comes with it?

Paul wanted to encourage Timothy that the gospel is the only answer for humankind. It's worth all the effort, the tiredness, the slog, the mockery, the persecution. He says to Timothy, and to us: don't avoid the gospel to avoid suffering, but share the gospel, whatever the cost.

And there will be a cost. It is inevitable that those who share the ministry of the gospel will suffer (verse 12). But in the midst of our suffering God promises us his grace and power, enabling us to endure.

Whenever we feel ashamed of the suffering or of standing up for the gospel, we need to take ourselves in hand and rehearse the gospel's unique and transforming truth. This is what Paul is doing in verses 9 and 10: 'He has saved us and called us to a holy life – not because of anything we have done but because of his own purpose and grace.' Our holy calling is by grace, not works, and was part of God's divine plan from the beginning of time. Jesus has 'brought life and immortality to light through the gospel'. With Christ the floodlights come on, and we see what it means to say that death has lost its sting, the grave has lost its power, and all in Christ have eternal life with him. And all this is 'through the appearing of our Saviour, Christ Jesus'. Our salvation is rooted, grounded and assured in Christ, because it's achieved by Christ.

This is the gospel! This is eternal truth. There is nothing to be ashamed of. We stand upon what God himself has done.

Are you suffering for the gospel? Not many of us face physical persecution, but there will be consequences if we let the gospel shape our decisions and values: strained relationships with non-Christian family members; being passed over for promotion because you don't indulge in office gossip; tiredness because you serve in church ministries during the week. If you are struggling in this area, tell yourself the gospel, remind yourself of its truth. Ask God to give you his grace and power as you serve him today.

Day 5

Read 2 Timothy 1:3–18
Key verse: 2 Timothy 1:12

....

12 That is why I am suffering as I am. Yet this is no cause for shame, because I know whom I have believed, and am convinced that he is able to guard what I have entrusted to him until that day.

What do you say to someone who is suffering for being a Christian? What do you say to yourself when you are suffering for the sake of the gospel?

Notice what Paul does. He lifts Timothy's eyes to Jesus. He encourages Timothy to look to Jesus who is the Lord of the gospel, and therefore the guarantor of the gospel.

The text does not say '*in* whom I believed' but '*whom* I believed'. '*In whom*' is an arm's-length relationship, but '*whom* I believed' speaks of a close, devoted relationship to Christ. How often have you seen people who after forty or fifty years in the church, by the grace of God, come to trust Christ for the first time? That is the movement from '*in whom*' to '*whom*'.

Knowing the Lord in this personal way is how our hearts are convinced of the gospel. We can be sure that although the world mocks and ignores Christianity, the gospel is for ever. It will be vindicated on the final day as the power of God for salvation. And because we know Jesus, we trust that 'he is able to guard what I have entrusted to him until that day'. Jesus will guard the truth of the gospel throughout the generations, because it is his gospel.

More than that, if we give ourselves to Jesus, we can be sure he will guard and keep us until the final day. This doesn't mean we'll avoid suffering and hardships, but it does mean that as we live faithfully for God, we don't need to worry about the results of our ministry or the outcome of our lives; we can leave those with him. We can trust him with all that is precious to us, knowing he is completely trustworthy.

Today, look to Jesus. It may be difficult for you to share the gospel or live out gospel values but, in God's strength, press on! One day you will be vindicated. It's Jesus' responsibility to preserve the gospel and he will do it! Our role is to live and serve him wholeheartedly. Stop worrying about results or what other people think of you. Don't let your suffering get in the way of living 'all out' for God. Entrust yourself totally to God's care and keeping. Trust him with the outcome of your life and service. Today, consciously live for 'an audience of One'.

Day 6

Read 2 Timothy 1:3–18
Key verses: 2 Timothy 1:13–14

. . . .

> [13] *What you heard from me, keep as the pattern of sound teaching, with faith and love in Christ Jesus.* [14] *Guard the good deposit that was entrusted to you – guard it with the help of the Holy Spirit who lives in us.*

What are the fundamentals, the non-negotiables, of our faith?

In verses 13 and 14, Paul gives us two commands: 'keep' and 'guard'. What we are to keep is 'the pattern of sound teaching'. 'The pattern' is like an architect's sketch, showing the main fabric of a building, not just the finishing touches. Paul is saying to Timothy that the foundations of the building are fixed for ever. They are non-negotiable. It is what is sometimes called the *kerygma* – that is, the central truths of the faith.

The truths of the gospel are living truths, brought about by Jesus Christ in his incarnation, atonement, resurrection and ascension, and by the Holy Spirit poured out upon the church. You cannot disagree or compromise on these fundamental facts of the gospel. Other things can be altered or disposed of; the external bricks of the building, such as leadership structures and worship styles, may vary. But the central girders and foundations are for ever!

And we are to 'guard' this gospel. Today, as always, there are attacks on the gospel. All Christians are called to be guardians of the faith. As people seek to subtract from it, add to it or alter it, we must hold on to it because it is the only gospel whereby people can be saved.

So how do we 'keep' and 'guard' the gospel? By reciting a creed or shouting slogans? No. We 'keep' and 'guard' the gospel when:

• we take Christ and his Word seriously, spending time studying and meditating on Scripture

• we daily live by gospel values with our faith and love in Jesus

• we rely on the love and power of the Holy Spirit in all we do.

Church is full of a variety of people, of different backgrounds, denominations, races, ages and genders. How can we work together? What binds us together when so much else divides? Christian unity is based on the core elements of the gospel which we are to build our lives on. This week, serve together with other Christian brothers and sisters. Whatever your differences, unite around the core truths of the gospel, and don't fall out over secondary issues. As we live out these gospel truths, we will face opposition. There will be temptation to 'dilute' the gospel or 'sugar coat' it. Today, ask the Holy Spirit for help to 'guard' the gospel in your family, workplace and even church, with God's love and grace.

Day 7

Read 2 Timothy 1:3–18
Key verses: 2 Timothy 1:15–18

....

¹⁵ *You know that everyone in the province of Asia has deserted me, including Phygelus and Hermogenes.*

¹⁶ May the Lord show mercy to the household of Onesiphorus, because he often refreshed me and was not ashamed of my chains. ¹⁷ On the contrary, when he was in Rome, he searched hard for me until he found me. ¹⁸ May the Lord grant that he will find mercy from the Lord on that day! You know very well in how many ways he helped me in Ephesus.

Think about the Christians who have made an impact on your life. What did they say? What did they do? What character traits most impressed you?

Paul had served God long enough to experience the disappointment as well as the joy of serving with other Christians. He was grieved when the believers in Asia deserted him. He mentions Phygelus and Hermogenes by name. Perhaps they were the ringleaders? We don't know anything about these two characters apart from their unfaithfulness – what a thing to be remembered for! Paul was deeply hurt by their unfaithfulness to him and the gospel.

But he was also greatly cheered by faithful Christians. He mentions Onesiphorus to Timothy. Onesiphorus searched him out on visits to Rome and keeps coming back. He and his household helped Paul in 'many ways'. The key verse is verse 16: 'he . . . was not ashamed of my chains.' Onesiphorus was an encouragement to Paul, who wants him to be an encouragement to Timothy too. Paul prays for this fellow worker and mentions him by name as an encouragement to Timothy not to be ashamed of Paul, the gospel, or of suffering for it.

Many of us have been on the receiving end of 'friendly fire'. Being let down and betrayed by other Christians is hard to deal with. Ask for God's help to forgive those who have hurt you and for his strength to move on. Thank God for the ways you have been encouraged by Christian friends; try to be specific! Today, think about the legacy you are leaving to other believers. When they watch your life, will they be encouraged by your loyalty to God? Will they see gospel values lived out? Will they see you faithfully serving other believers for the extension of God's kingdom? Could you be like an Onesiphorus to them?

Day 8

Read 2 Timothy 2:1–13
Key verse: 2 Timothy 2:1

. . . .

¹You then, my son, be strong in the grace that is in Christ Jesus.

Have you ever read a Christian biography and thought, 'That could never happen to me' or 'God could never work in my life like that'? Sometimes we struggle to believe God is able to work through us.

Paul is about to die. The thought of being without him must have been overwhelming for Timothy. But Paul's response is unequivocal: 'You then, my son, be strong in the grace that is in Christ Jesus. You are stepping into the breach, and you are to prove the God of Paul to be the same God for Timothy, and for every Christian.'

I had to wrestle with this idea when I was preparing to preach a sermon series on Moses. Do I believe that the God who brought Moses out of Egypt, crossing the Red

Sea and taking all those people through the wilderness, is the same God I worship through Christ Jesus? If I do, then I cannot go on acting as though I am cooped up in the wilderness with no way through it. He is my God.

There are lots of people who have been converted but who are still living off other people's experiences. They are dependent on a famous preacher or their church minister. They have never moved into that position where they themselves draw on the grace of Christ. God bids Timothy to move into that position, and prove 'the grace that is in Christ Jesus'.

He commands him to 'be strong' and 'be strengthened'; the expression can be used both ways. As we hunger for God, he meets us in grace and strength. If we don't abide in him and he in us, we remain weak, like hungry people sitting at a banqueting table too lazy to reach out for food; like thirsty people lying by a fountain, too lazy to reach out and drink. We have so many resources to help us grow as Christians. The food is all around us, the fountain is around us; feed and drink.

There are great Bible texts on this theme. 'I can do all this through him who gives me strength' (Philippians 4:13), or 'Be strong in the Lord . . . so that you can take your stand against the devil's schemes' (Ephesians 6:10–11), or 'My grace is sufficient for you, for my power is made perfect in weakness' (2 Corinthians 12:9). Our weakness is no excuse. God revels in our weakness, as it shows his strength. I believe that it's vitally important for Christians to rediscover the pounding theme of the New Testament: that it is in Christ that you find your strength.

But 'being strong in the grace of God' doesn't mean just waiting until you're strong enough to go out; it's about going out into the waters and finding that they recede. It's when you put your foot forward that the power of God enables you. If you wait until you feel strong enough to serve, you'll wait for ever.

God wants to work through you! He is not just the God of Paul or Timothy, your parents or your minister. He is your God and he wants you to experience his grace. Don't settle for someone else's spiritual leftovers. Feed on God for yourself. Think about the books you read, the music you listen to, the TV you watch. Are they nourishing your soul? When you are connected to God, you will experience his strength in your life. Don't believe the lie that your weakness disqualifies you from service – it is a prerequisite! Our weakness is the backdrop for God to display his strength. So be strong in God's grace and step out in service.

Day 9

Read 2 Timothy 2:1–13
Key verse: 2 Timothy 2:2

....

²And the things you have heard me say in the presence of many witnesses entrust to reliable people who will also be qualified to teach others.

Do you struggle to discern God's will? What university should I attend, what career should I choose, when should I retire, where should I live?

Sometimes it's difficult to work out what God wants us to do. But one thing we can be certain of: wherever we live, work or study, God wants us to teach the gospel to others. The principle is to teach others, who can teach others, who can teach others, ad infinitum. If that strategy had not been followed, you would not be a Christian. The strategy of the Christian church, throughout the New Testament, is to train people who can train others.

Paul explains, 'The things you have heard me say' – the apostle is handing on the apostolic truth – 'in the presence of many witnesses'. We believe that the central truths of the Christian faith are truths which have been hammered out before witnesses. Paul was not handing on some secret tradition, which you had to be in the inner circle to know. Before many witnesses, God broke into the world and showed his glory. He worked out his saving purpose not in a corner, but on the public stage of the world.

And Timothy must entrust the gospel to 'reliable people'. If you entrust this truth to unreliable people, it is destroyed or twisted. If they hand it on to others, it becomes more twisted and distorted until people are destroyed. Jesus demonstrated this principle of teaching reliable people who could entrust the good news to others. He withdrew from public ministry after the halfway point of his own work, to teach the Twelve, to concentrate on explaining and deepening their understanding. He could have spent his time preaching and performing miracles for the crowds. Instead, he sat down with the Twelve and trained them. That is why, when he went back to glory, the church went forward in the power of the Spirit.

God is committed to the gospel and he wants all of us to be involved in passing his truth on to the next generation. Whatever else we're involved in, this is God's will for each of us. Unfortunately, most of us are like sheep: only interested in what's in front of our nose! When you have your nose down on the immediate things, you lose sight of the greater purposes in which you are taking part. God says to us today, 'Come on, get your head up. Realize who you are; realize the greater purposes into which I have called you. Head up! Head up!'

Life is full of pressing decisions and we want to follow God's will at every stage. But look up! You are part of God's story of salvation. He has a great purpose planned for you which doesn't depend on geography or your stage of life. You are called to share the gospel with others, to teach and train them up in God's truth. Whom are you training? Your children, grandchildren, a younger person at church, a work colleague? Ask God to give you opportunities to pass on the baton of faith. Lift your head up and delight in the great purpose God has in mind for you.

Day 10

Read 2 Timothy 2:1–13
Key verses: 2 Timothy 2:3–4

....

[3] Join with me in suffering, like a good soldier of Christ Jesus. [4] No one serving as a soldier gets entangled in civilian affairs, but rather tries to please his commanding officer.

Consider the choices you are making, the priorities you have, the relationships in which you are investing. Do you think Jesus is pleased with them? Is he pleased with how you are living?

Paul sees himself as a soldier whose aim is 'to please his commanding officer' (verse 4). One translation says the soldier's goal is to be 'always at the commanding officer's disposal'. It is a personal aim. Paul echoes this sentiment in 2 Corinthians 5:9: 'We make it our goal to please him.'

Of course, we please Christ by obeying him. Christ wants us to have unquestioning allegiance to his authority. A good soldier is one who says, 'Your will be done.' Saying this to God is the deepest expression of our faith. How else can you explain Gethsemane? In agony, with sweat falling from his face like drops of blood, Jesus was obeying his Father.

Tragically, some Christians treat God like a genie in the bottle. You rub the lamp, and the genie appears and says, 'Yes, Master, what do you want?' But in the New Testament it is the other way around. Of course God is there to meet us in saving grace and love. That is the glory of being in his family. But commitment means coming to him and saying, 'Yes, Master, what do *you* want?'

Saying 'Your will be done' involves a readiness to suffer. So verse 3 says, 'Join with me in suffering, like a good soldier of Christ Jesus.' God is looking for men and women who rule nothing out, who are willing to go wherever, and do whatever, he asks, regardless of the suffering involved.

If you are going to be committed in this way, you cannot be 'entangled in civilian affairs'. The word in Greek is *empleko*, from which we get our word 'implicated'. It's like when your hair gets so knotty you can't get a comb through it. God is not asking us to avoid family responsibilities or never enjoy hobbies; these are important. He means we must not be so entangled that we cannot go where, and do what, our commanding officer requires.

Is it your goal to please God?

Bring to God all the situations and issues with which you are struggling. Stop wrestling. Stop trying to manipulate the outcome. Stop trying to fix things. Imagine writing over each of these scenarios, '**Your will be done**.' Gladly submit your will to God's in each circumstance. As you go through your day, accept from God's hand the suffering that comes with obedience. But also enjoy the freedom that comes from not having to please everyone else. Let your soul delight in having a single focus to pursue. Our sole aim, our single passion, is to please God.

Day 11

Read 2 Timothy 2:1–13
Key verse: 2 Timothy 2:5

. . . .

⁵Similarly, anyone who competes as an athlete does not receive the victor's crown except by competing according to the rules.

If you had to describe your spiritual life, what image would you choose? I imagine that not many of us would describe ourselves as athletes straining towards godliness!

But Paul encourages us that we have a race to run and it has to be 'according to the rules'. In the ancient Olympic Games, the athletes had to swear on oath that they had undergone constant training for ten months – these were the rules.

Not many Christians show that degree of determination. Most of us find it difficult to snatch a quick quiet time before we go off to work. But athletes are a graphic illustration of the dedication we must devote to our own spiritual training. Runners who practise, whatever the weather, to reach the finishing line and obtain the prize. Swimmers who get up at five in the morning to swim for two or three hours while the pool is quiet.

If you are serious about your commitment to Christ, you will want to pursue the holiness that is vital to the Christian race. In 1 Corinthians 9:24–27, Paul talks about the strict training of spirit, mind and body he engaged in:

> [24]Do you not know that in a race all the runners run, but only one gets the prize? Run in such a way as to get the prize. [25]Everyone who competes in the games goes into strict training. They do it to get a crown that will not last; but we do it to get a crown that will last forever. [26]Therefore I do not run like someone running aimlessly; I do not fight like a boxer beating the air. [27]No, I strike a blow to my body and make it my slave so that after I have preached to others, I myself will not be disqualified for the prize.

If we want to receive a crown that will last forever, then a determined pursuit of holiness is not a luxury but a necessity. Devote yourself like an athlete to your spiritual training. Daily, set aside time to read the Bible and pray. Ask the Holy Spirit to help you say 'no' to sin and 'yes' to what pleases God. Meet up with other believers to spur one another on. Keep pressing on!

For most of us, the Christian race is not a sprint but a marathon. At many points along life's course, we lose sight of the prize and get tired or discouraged. We could have avoided this gruelling pursuit of holiness if God had instantly transformed us to be like his Son. God could have done that, but he chose not to. Instead, he wants to partner with us. He wants us to learn to rely on him, to trust him and yield ourselves to him more fully. He wants us to experience the joy of wholehearted devotion and the Holy Spirit's enabling power. Perhaps you have let your spiritual training lapse. Don't give up; get your running shoes back on! Keep your eye on the prize and look forward to God cheering you on to the finishing line, saying, 'Well done, good and faithful servant'.

Day 12

Read 2 Timothy 2:1–13
Key verses: 2 Timothy 2:6–7

. . . .

> *⁶The hardworking farmer should be the first to receive a share of the crops. ⁷Reflect on what I am saying, for the Lord will give you insight into all this.*

Church is often compared to a football match: twenty-two people doing all the work and everyone else sitting watching them! But being a Christian is never a spectator sport.

In verse 6, Paul gives us the picture of a farmer. There's little glamour or excitement in farming. A farmer labours in all weathers. He works relentlessly in the lashing rain, the gale-force winds and even the dark winter mornings.

In the same way, although it's a wonderful privilege to serve Christ, it's also hard work. It's an effort to go out to the prayer meeting after a long day in the office; it's usually a thankless task to be on the rota for the church sound system; it's not thrilling to prepare meals for Alpha or Christianity Explored. Most of the ways in which we serve Christ are not glamorous or exciting, just hard work.

Paul describes his own commitment to the gospel as 'sowing', 'watering', 'reaping', 'pioneering', 'contending' and 'defending'. Like a farmer, he has worked tirelessly in all circumstances.

But though the work is hard, we will be rewarded. 'The hardworking farmer should be the first to receive a share of the crops.' This doesn't mean financial remuneration, but we'll be rewarded with joy as we see the gospel change lives. We'll see the results of our efforts as people are transformed by the good news.

So Paul says to Timothy and to us, 'Reflect on what I am saying.' Reflect on the images of the soldier, athlete and farmer. Acknowledge the dedication required to serve Christ and joyfully persevere, knowing that he and the gospel are worth it.

Are you working hard for God? If your answer is 'no', think about what God requires of you. How does he want you to serve him at church, work or in your family? If you are already working hard for God, don't waste time seeking praise or thanks; this is the way life is meant to be! Instead, focus on your reward. Think how the gospel is bearing fruit in the lives around you. It's true that we won't always see the difference our service for God is making. But in heaven our reward will be on display for all to see. There will be people there because you shared the gospel with them, you provided a meal at an Alpha course, you prayed for a missionary's work overseas. Hard work now guarantees friends in heaven later!

Day 13

Read 2 Timothy 2:1–13
Key verses: 2 Timothy 2:8–10

....

⁸Remember Jesus Christ, raised from the dead, descended from David. This is my gospel, ⁹for which I am suffering even to the point of being chained like a criminal. But God's word is not chained. ¹⁰Therefore I endure everything for the sake of the elect, that they too may obtain the salvation that is in Christ Jesus, with eternal glory.

Think about the Christians you admire most. What impresses you about these people? What character traits stand out?

In these verses and throughout the New Testament, endurance is praised as a key character quality. Peter talked about endurance in the context of persecution (1 Peter 2:20). The apostle James knew the importance of it (James 5:11). While this epistle was being written, John called for the endurance of the saints, 'those who keep

God's commands and hold fast their testimony about Jesus' (Revelation 12:17).

Paul too, 'chained like a criminal', endured for the sake of Christ. He endured prison knowing that many of the Praetorian Guard trusted Christ because of his witness (Philippians 1:13). As he reminded the Corinthians, endurance was one of the ways to serve the Lord:

> As servants of God we commend ourselves in every way: in great endurance; in troubles, hardships and distresses; in beatings, imprisonments and riots; in hard work, sleepless nights and hunger.
> (2 Corinthians 6:4–5)

Endurance literally means to stay behind, not to run away when the fight is on. Another word for endurance would be 'stickability'. Jesus himself understood what it meant to endure, and that's why Paul urges us, 'Remember Jesus Christ': 'For the joy that was set before him he [Jesus] endured the cross, scorning its shame, and sat down at the right hand of the throne of God' (Hebrews 12:2).

We are called to endure in the heat and pain of suffering for the gospel. Our endurance is the background against which people will come to faith as the gospel is preached. Paul wouldn't have endured the suffering if he didn't believe that the gospel was supremely worth the cost.

Nor would he have been content to be in prison if that had stopped the gospel spreading. But he was convinced that 'God's word is not chained'.

This great truth burnt in Paul's heart and helped him to endure. May it burn in ours.

God's Word is not chained. It will do its work in:

- antagonistic offices

- Islamic countries

- atheist universities

- uninterested friends and family.

So don't despise your chains! You can't begin to imagine how God will use your suffering to spread his love and hope to others. Let God do his work. In the meantime, keep enduring. Live out the gospel with your eyes fixed on Jesus. He endured to save you and he uses your endurance to save others. What a plan!

Day 14

Read 2 Timothy 2:1–13
Key verses: 2 Timothy 2:11–13

. . . .

¹¹ Here is a trustworthy saying:

If we died with him,
*   we will also live with him;*
¹² if we endure,
*   we will also reign with him.*
If we disown him,
*   he will also disown us;*
¹³ if we are faithless,
*   he remains faithful,*
*   for he cannot disown himself.*

Life looks better when we have something to look forward to. We can cope with hospital appointments, exams and our daily routine if we know we have a holiday, a meal out with friends, or even a favourite TV programme to look forward to.

With these verses from an early Christian hymn, Paul encourages us to persevere in our suffering, because we have something to look forward to. Jesus will return soon and take us home to heaven. We can die to self and submit ourselves to God now, because we know heaven is on the horizon. We can endure suffering for the gospel, knowing that one day soon we will reign with God for ever.

Of course God is faithful to his warnings as well as his promises, because he cannot deny himself. So, 'If we disown him, he will also disown us.' Jesus himself made this point clear in Matthew 10:32–33: 'Whoever acknowledges me before others, I will also acknowledge before my Father in heaven. But whoever disowns me before others, I will disown before my Father in heaven.' Jesus is talking about those who persistently refuse to acknowledge his sovereignty. Parables like the foolish virgins and the unfaithful steward in Matthew 25 encourage us to nail our colours to the mast, to live faithfully for God now, ready for Christ's return.

Of course there will be times, even as Christians, when we fail God. But thank God that his commitment to us is not based on our fickle character or our performance. God's faithfulness to us is based on his own unchanging and perfect character. Because we can trust his character, we can hold on to his promises and endure through difficult days, waiting confidently for heaven.

Read Revelation 4, 5, 21 and 22. Let your mind wander as you imagine what heaven will be like. Much of the time we are too satisfied with life here to think about heaven. But get into the habit of thinking each day about heaven. Keep your eyes on the reality that awaits us, the heavenly city we shall one day call 'home'. Let the thoughts of heaven give you an eternal perspective on your failure, suffering and heartbreak. Let the reality of heaven shape your choices and priorities now. Let the certainty of heaven give you strength to endure until the very end.

Day 15

Read 2 Timothy 2:14–19
Key verse: 2 Timothy 2:14

....

> ¹⁴ *Keep reminding God's people of these things. Warn them before God against quarrelling about words; it is of no value, and only ruins those who listen.*

Every now and again, a fad infiltrates the church. Discernment goes out the window and we are caught up with some overemphasis of an aspect of Christian truth. We are swept along by the crowds and our love of the spectacular. Often these secondary issues are promoted by brilliant communication, money and publicity. It is easy to start believing that this single issue is all that really matters.

Paul has seen this happen before and he is concerned that we are able to discern between truth and secondary matters. He has seen the damage that these senseless controversies cause, the danger of holding a form of religion but denying its power, and the insidious nature of counterfeit faith. We are not to play games like this when we bring the gospel to the world.

Paul cautions against 'quarrelling about words'. This is when we allow the minutiae to absorb a totally disproportionate amount of time and energy. We judge other Christians by whether or not they give importance to, and a particular interpretation of, this issue. Paul warns that this type of quarrelling only 'ruins those who listen'. The word used here can be translated 'catastrophe'. It is catastrophic for a Christian to pursue some secondary issue as the thing that matters above all else.

The quality that we need is discernment.

Think about the issues that cause controversy in your church. What topics do you and your friends discuss? Are you majoring on the minors? Are you 'quarrelling about words' and letting the minutiae absorb all your time and effort? Ask God for forgiveness. Pray that he will give you discernment so that you can devote yourself to what really matters in his kingdom. Take care how you use your words at home, at work and in your family. Words are more powerful than we realize; we can use them to tear people down or build them up.

Pray that the conversations you have this week with other Christians are edifying and encouraging: 'Let us consider how we may spur one another on towards love and good deeds' (Hebrews 10:24).

Day 16

Read 2 Timothy 2:14–19
Key verse: 2 Timothy 2:15

....

15Do your best to present yourself to God as one approved, a worker who does not need to be ashamed and who correctly handles the word of truth.

Do you feel far away from God, indifferent to his commands and distracted by all that's going on around you? Sometimes we wonder why God isn't speaking to us, why we can't hear his voice. Often the answer is simple: we are not spending time in his Word.

God speaks to us in various ways, but primarily through the Bible. If we want to know God's priorities, wisdom, commands and promises, we need to read the Bible. It is not always easy to understand what is written or how to apply it to our contexts. However, like diligent workers, we must invest time and effort in our study.

For pastors and teachers, the responsibility is immense. The teaching of God's Word must be their central task.

They must give it priority in terms of time and energy. The aim of their preaching is not to entertain or please us. God's approval is what counts. But Paul's charge is not just to pastors. This verse applies to all of us. It is vital that we 'correctly handle the word of truth', in a way God approves.

The word that Paul uses for 'handling' literally means 'cutting a straight road'. Remember that this is what John the Baptist had to do to prepare people for Jesus' coming. The prophecy about John was that he would 'Prepare the way for the Lord, make straight paths for him' (Mark 1:3). He was to level the hills and fill the valleys in preparation for Jesus' coming. In other words, his role was to prepare a straight clear road so that Jesus could have access.

This is what each of us must do. We must 'handle' God's Word in such a way that we prepare a straight road for the Lord to move on. Our job is to dig and dig and compare and ponder and meditate and pray and plumb the amazing depths of the Word. Whenever we read the Bible, for ourselves or to teach it to others, our task is to cut a straight road: the straight road of truth. The goal is for Christ to have clear and unhindered access to our hearts.

Are you giving God room to move? Are you spending time reading the Bible, making the path straight for the Holy Spirit to speak to you? Are you removing sin and other obstacles, and giving God direct access to your heart?

Think about any Bible teaching that you do. Could God put his stamp of approval on your ministry? Would God approve of the way you handle his Word when you teach others – not manipulating it to say what you want it to say, but allowing it to speak for itself? Are you putting roadblocks in the way of God's truth, or are you cutting a straight road for him to speak to others?

Day 17

Read 2 Timothy 2:14–19
Key verses: 2 Timothy 2:16–19

....

¹⁶Avoid godless chatter, because those who indulge in it will become more and more ungodly. ¹⁷Their teaching will spread like gangrene. Among them are Hymenaeus and Philetus, ¹⁸who have departed from the truth. They say that the resurrection has already taken place, and they destroy the faith of some. ¹⁹Nevertheless, God's solid foundation stands firm, sealed with this inscription: 'The Lord knows those who are his,' and, 'Everyone who confesses the name of the Lord must turn away from wickedness.'

'The Lord knows those who are his' – what comforting words! The fact that God has intimate knowledge and a personal relationship with those who belong to him is certainly a truth to cling on to in difficult times.

Paul is dealing with false teaching, which he describes as 'godless chatter'. It is godless because it has nothing to do with the truth of God. This chatter leads people into more and more ungodliness, further and further away from God and his holiness.

The issue seems to have been that Hymenaeus and Philetus, leading members of the church, were teaching that the 'resurrection had already taken place'. These two had 'departed from the truth', yet strangely they still seem to have been Christian leaders. Look what the result is: 'they destroy the faith of some' (verse 18). Their false teaching spread like gangrene.

Paul cautions us to avoid such heresy, to 'turn away from wickedness'. Don't be upset by the godless chatter and false teaching even of leading churchmen. Instead, be strong in your own faith and focus on God's promises: 'God's solid foundation stands firm, sealed with this inscription: "The Lord knows those who are his." '

God assures us that his church, which upholds his truth, is a solid foundation. Paul's quote in verse 19, 'The Lord knows those who are his', is taken from Numbers 16:5 and Korah's revolt against Moses and Aaron. False teachers were challenging their ministry, and these are Moses' words of challenge to the people. Paul uses Moses' quote to remind us that God is the arbiter. It is God's church, and he knows who are his.

Whatever attacks the church faces, either from within or from without, Jesus has promised, 'I will build my church, and the gates of Hades will not overcome it' (Matthew 16:18). The church's future and security are protected by God, and he knows each one who is his.

The church is God's best idea. As Paul explained to the Ephesian believers, it was God's way of displaying his wisdom for all to see. But as the church faces wave after wave of false teaching, it's easy to become disillusioned. It is bewildering to know the wisest way to oppose the godlessness that subtly infiltrates the body of Christ. Don't waste time being disappointed in church leaders or getting sucked into the heresy. Trust God's promise that he has a future for the church. He will protect and sustain it. Pray for your church and its leaders. Pray that you would stay faithful to God's Word and be a source of truth and light in this present darkness.

Day 18

Read 2 Timothy 2:20–26
Key verses: 2 Timothy 2:20–21

. . . .

20 In a large house there are articles not only of gold and silver, but also of wood and clay; some are for special purposes and some for common use. 21 Those who cleanse themselves from the latter will be instruments for special purposes, made holy, useful to the Master and prepared to do any good work.

How holy is your life? We may have lots of good qualities and gifts. We may be hard-working, discerning and determined, but if we are not holy, God can't use us.

To help us understand this, Paul describes the image of a house. We are the house and Jesus is the Master. You and I are not our own; we are bought with a price. If we surrender to Christ, he enters our life as Master.

Imagine Fred's fish and chip shop. It has been on the high street for many years. The greasy wallpaper and cracked lino hasn't been changed since the 1990s. Then one day, to everyone's surprise, there is a banner across the window: 'Under new management'. It becomes Fred's fish restaurant. Fred is still there, but he is no longer in charge; he's an employee. The new owner goes round the building pointing out to Fred all the bits that need to be changed. The old tables are thrown out, new wallpaper put on, more lights set up – which immediately shows up more to be cleaned!

It's the same place, but it has undergone a transformation. It is the same when Christ enters our life. He can only come as owner-manager. Across our life goes the label 'Under new management', and immediately he has access to every part of our life. Nothing is outside his gaze. He immediately puts his finger on the things that need changing. And as he brings more light, so we see more that needs to be changed.

The cleaning process begins with a major spring clean. To use Jesus' terminology in John 13, we first have a bath and then the constant foot-washing follows. So verse 21 is concerned with purifying. We are made clean by the Word (John 15), by confession of sin (1 John 1), by asking for washing and renewal (Psalm 51). We must take action about the things that we know to be a major offence to God. This is an ongoing process. The Christian who has a conversion experience but doesn't go in for foot-washing (constant purification) backslides. We have to go on and on, cleaning, purifying, washing, and wrestling with the inner nature which disgraces God. Then God can use us.

Have you washed your feet recently? I'm not talking about the big bath of your conversion. Today, have you confessed your sin and asked God to wash you through his Word? Keep short accounts with God; come to him daily for forgiveness. Don't be discouraged: it will be a constant battle to stay clean. The more God shines his light on every part of your life and the more you clean up your heart, the more the dirty stains stand out! Being aware of your sin and the need to repent is actually a good sign. It means that the owner of our house is making progress with the transformation!

Day 19

Read 2 Timothy 2:20–26
Key verse: 2 Timothy 2:22

....

²² Flee the evil desires of youth and pursue righteousness, faith, love and peace, along with those who call on the Lord out of a pure heart.

Are you the only Christian in your office or your family? At times, being a Christian can be an isolating experience. But Paul encourages us to remember that we are never alone in our pursuit of holiness.

There is strength and encouragement to be gathered from belonging to a Christian community. Church provides fellowship, it grounds us, it helps us persevere, knowing we are running the Christian race 'along with those who call on the Lord out of a pure heart'.

There is both a positive and negative aspect to our pursuit of holiness. On the one hand, we are to 'Flee the evil desires of youth'. A sexual relationship in the context of committed married love is a beautiful thing and a gift of God. But outside of marriage it is sin. The word 'flee' means to 'run away'. Remember Joseph? He ran from the house when Potiphar's wife tried to trap him. The cost was prison, misunderstanding and accusation, but he did the right thing. We need to flee from youthful passions, to put distance between ourselves and temptation.

This is true for all of us, but it is vital for ministers and church leaders. In 1 Timothy 3:9, Paul says that deacons 'must keep hold of the deep truths of the faith with a clear conscience'. If you are in church leadership, don't get caught out by sexual sin or temptation; make sure you keep your conscience clear.

The other aspect of holiness is to 'pursue righteousness, faith, love and peace'. Thankfully, we don't have to do this in our own strength. The Holy Spirit not only exposes the wrong in our lives, but also develops the fruit of the Spirit in us.

Draw strength from the Holy Spirit and the support of your Christian brothers and sisters as you pursue holiness today.

Imagine yourself running the race of faith. Look around and see the 'great cloud of witnesses' (Hebrews 12:1) cheering you on – heroes from the Bible, perhaps members of your family, church friends, the person who led you to Christ. Notice that this is not a solo race; many others are running alongside you. How can you spur them on? How can you help one another practically to 'flee the evil desires of youth and pursue righteousness'? Start by being authentic: be honest about your struggles, willing to receive godly advice, generous with your encouragement, and determined to seek one another's good. Support one another practically and prayerfully as you see the finish line come into view.

Day 20

Read 2 Timothy 2:20–26
Key verses: 2 Timothy 2:23–26

. . . .

23 Don't have anything to do with foolish and stupid arguments, because you know they produce quarrels. 24 And the Lord's servant must not be quarrelsome but must be kind to everyone, able to teach, not resentful. 25 Opponents must be gently instructed, in the hope that God will grant them repentance leading them to a knowledge of the truth, 26 and that they will come to their senses and escape from the trap of the devil, who has taken them captive to do his will.

How do we share the gospel with people? In our generation, when there is so much opposition and apathy, how do we win people for Christ?

As God's servant, we should be 'kind to everyone'. This phrase is only used one other time in the New Testament, in 1 Thessalonians 2:7. Here Paul says, 'We were gentle among you, like a nurse taking care of her children' (RSV). The nurse's chief priority is the patient. He or she is not diverted by minor issues. Similarly, in evangelism, we must not be distracted by the many other issues which matter to us. We are not to be 'quarrelsome' (verse 24) and we are to avoid 'foolish and stupid arguments' (verse 23). We must watch our attitudes, behaviour and speech so that there is nothing about us which is a barrier to the gospel.

A nurse is gentle and kind and goes very carefully with people. If a bottle of medicine is labelled 'one tablet per day', a nurse doesn't say, 'Well, I'm going to speed up your recovery. Take the whole lot.' And in verse 25 Paul reminds us that 'opponents must be gently instructed'. You don't win people by violent reactions or by mocking them. You win them by patience, love and correcting them with gentleness. The false teachers of 2 Timothy 2 are won back to the truth by love and care, not by condemnation or confrontation.

Sharing the gospel means that we listen to people. We spend time with them, often over many months, carefully and patiently helping them to understand what is involved in becoming a Christian. Our role is to prepare the way for God by teaching, loving and nursing so that he in his mercy may perhaps 'grant them repentance'.

Understanding and obeying God's Word is the only way that people can escape 'the trap of the devil'. The picture here is that of becoming sober after being drunk or drugged. The world's way of thinking and its standards act like a drug, ensnaring us into the devil's net. But it is our privilege to share God's truth with patience, gentleness, skill and love, and to watch friends, family and colleagues find true freedom in Christ.

Think of the non-Christians God has placed in your life: the friend you meet at the gym, the work colleague, the parent at the school gate, your grandchildren. God has given you these people to love and gently share the gospel with. Your life and speech are to be a demonstration of the gospel to them. What a privilege and responsibility! Choose five people in your sphere of influence who aren't Christians. Commit to pray for them daily. Pray for opportunities to speak to them about Christ, to demonstrate his love, and ask the Holy Spirit to work in their hearts to draw them to faith.

Day 21

Read 2 Timothy 3:1–17
Key verses: 2 Timothy 3:10–13

....

¹⁰*You, however, know all about my teaching, my way of life, my purpose, faith, patience, love, endurance, ¹¹persecutions, sufferings – what kinds of things happened to me in Antioch, Iconium and Lystra, the persecutions I endured. Yet the Lord rescued me from all of them. ¹²In fact, everyone who wants to live a godly life in Christ Jesus will be persecuted, ¹³while evildoers and impostors will go from bad to worse, deceiving and being deceived.*

How do you feel when yet another scandal about the church hits the headlines?

Paul reminds us that there is no point in getting anxious or distressed. From the beginning, there has been worldliness in the church. It is not new for people to be 'lovers of themselves' and 'lovers of money' (2 Timothy 3:2). Consumerism and materialism have always been prevalent.

Sadly, it's common for family life to be warped by ingratitude, unholiness, inhumanity, unforgiveness and children's disobedience.

Many are 'lovers of pleasure rather than lovers of God' (2 Timothy 3:4); they fit God in, but not as Lord. The worthlessness of nominal Christianity is revealed as people hold 'a form of godliness but deny its power' (2 Timothy 3:5). In verses 6 and 7, Paul shares an example of a group of weak women who idolize an influential person in the church, but never accept the truth of the gospel for themselves. In verse 8, he points to false teachers in the church with corrupt minds and counterfeit faith.

How do we respond to this bleak picture? Paul urges us to meet it with an unswerving commitment to teaching and living truth: 'Do your best to present yourself to God as one approved, a worker who does not need to be ashamed and who correctly handles the word of truth' (2 Timothy 2:15).

Paul calls us to follow his example. He didn't run after every false trail. Instead, he persevered with sound teaching, holy conduct and a godly purpose. He practised faith, patience, love and endurance. He accepted persecutions and sufferings as inevitable in the life of God.

He ploughed a straight furrow and cut a clear road. Whatever else was going on in the church, he clung to the truths of the gospel and lived them out.

There has always been worldliness in the church. But don't let worldly leaders or their practices become a role model for you. Don't get sucked into copying what's going on around you. Instead, look for godly examples to follow, people like Paul who preached the gospel and lived it out regardless of the suffering. But best of all, keep your eyes on Christ. Let his priorities set the standard for you, his example shape your life and his return help you persevere in this most holy faith.

Day 22

Read 2 Timothy 3:1–17
Key verses: 2 Timothy 3:14–15

....

¹⁴But as for you, continue in what you have learned and have become convinced of, because you know those from whom you learned it, ¹⁵and how from infancy you have known the Holy Scriptures, which are able to make you wise for salvation through faith in Christ Jesus.

How often do you read the Bible? It doesn't matter how long you've been a Christian or what ministry you are involved in; we all need to spend time in the Scriptures. It's fundamental to our faith.

After wrestling with all the sidetracks, godless chatter and worldliness in society and the church, Paul urges Timothy to turn back to Scripture. The word translated as 'continue' means settling in permanently. It's the word you use when you arrive where you are going to live, where you're going to unpack. The context suggests that Timothy's faith may have been rocked by the swirling influences around him. Of course, it's easy to be tossed about by theological debates, to be swept along by something new or to allow worldliness to seep into the church. As a countermeasure, Paul urges us to settle in God's Word permanently.

Coming back to Scripture meant coming home for Timothy, because that was how he had been brought up. From childhood he had 'known' the Scriptures. He had been taught about Abraham, Sarah, Moses, Esther, Paul and all the many thousands of millions of those who make up the family of God.

But even if we haven't been brought up in a Christian family, there is still the challenge to 'continue in what you have learned'. The Scriptures make us 'wise for salvation', but their usefulness doesn't stop there. Our goal must be to study the Bible in order to grasp the foundational truths of the Christian faith. This is more than just academic learning. God wants us to live out these truths by the power of the Holy Spirit. It's a lifelong process and an ongoing cycle. As we become more and more 'convinced' of the truth about God, we increasingly learn to trust his Word and rely on his resources to serve and witness. And, not surprisingly, as we live in the good of God's Word, we become more and more convinced that he is trustworthy!

You will never exhaust the Bible and you'll never outgrow it. From the moment you become a Christian until the end of life's race, it is your light, your strength, your manual for living and your ultimate authority. There is no deviation and no graduation, because we never move on from this core element of the faith. Daily time spent with God in his Word is not a luxury but a necessity. It's what you need to keep yourself centred in God, grounded in his truth and aware of his presence. Take care to set aside time to read the Bible this week. Make it a priority to cultivate this godly habit.

Day 23

Read 2 Timothy 3:1–17
Key verses: 2 Timothy 3:14–15

....

> [14] *But as for you, continue in what you have learned and have become convinced of, because you know those from whom you learned it,* [15] *and how from infancy you have known the Holy Scriptures, which are able to make you wise for salvation through faith in Christ Jesus.*

When young people look at you, are they attracted to your faith? Do they see you working out your faith, with a testimony of commitment, love, worship and joy? Are they inspired by you?

Look again at verses 14–15. Here Paul encourages Timothy to press on in his faith because 'you know those from whom you learned it'. Timothy's discipleship began in his family with his mother Eunice and grandmother Lois (2 Timothy 1:5). He witnessed their 'sincere faith', not just in Bible reading and church attendance, but also in the way they lived, relaxed, shared and enjoyed life. It seems likely Timothy's father was an unbeliever, but Timothy watched these two women living for God in good times and bad. Their faith had a deep impact on him.

Timothy could also look to Paul, not only as a teacher of the truth, but as a demonstrator of that truth in his own life. There can be no doubt of Paul's faith. His life was a glowing testimony of his commitment, love, worship and joy.

It's a great tragedy when churches have some cantankerous old people in them who are a disgrace to the gospel. It's damaging when young people can't look to senior Christians in the church and see them on fire for Christ. The greatest contribution that any older Christian can make to the church is to be a glowing example to the young people. Don't allow yourself to be weighed down by bitterness, resentment or disappointment. Instead, determine to trust God with whatever happens in life and press on to Christlikeness. Make your life and faith worth imitating. Choose to leave a legacy of godliness that is an example to those who follow after you.

What spiritual legacy are you leaving? When your children or the young folk in church look at your life, what do they see? For Timothy's mother, life could not have been easy, yet Timothy could see her faith shine.

Her trust in God made an indelible impression on his young heart. We can teach young people the truths of the faith, but unless our 'walk' matches up to our 'talk', it won't have any impact. Or rather, it will have a negative impact as our hypocrisy turns them off Christianity. Ask God to help you have integrity: your private thoughts matching your public actions. Pray that you'll be a godly example. This doesn't mean people won't see our flaws and failures, but they will also notice our repentance and our active desire to become more and more like Christ.

Day 24

Read 2 Timothy 3:1–17
Key verses: 2 Timothy 3:16–17

....

16All Scripture is God-breathed and is useful for teaching, rebuking, correcting and training in right-eousness, 17so that the servant of God may be thoroughly equipped for every good work.

Sometimes we treat God's Word like a bag of pick 'n' mix; we choose the verses we like and ignore the rest. Sometimes we try to manipulate Bible verses so that they say what we would like them to say. In essence, many of us are acting as if the Bible is only partly inspired by God, or perhaps not inspired at all!

But Paul explains that 'All Scripture is God-breathed' through the personalities and characters of people: the poets, the historians, the prophets, the psalmists. However, the emphasis here is that God is the initiator. Scripture is from the mind of God, by his Spirit, in his words or, in a quotation attributed to Gregory the Great,

Bishop of Rome in 684, 'The heart of God is in the words of God.'

It is not just the truth that validates Scripture; it is our experience of it. The fact that the Scriptures are constantly an inspiration to me confirms that they are the Word of God. You can turn back again and again to the Word and hear God speak to you through it. Some believers have tried to make a distinction between the Word and the Spirit, and have said, 'The only thing that matters to us is the experience of Christ, not the Bible.' But this is a false dichotomy – we experience Christ through the Scriptures!

J. B. Phillips was not an evangelical when he started translating the New Testament. He worked simply as a translator. But his experience of God in the Bible was profound. He said, 'Translating the New Testament was like rewiring a house with the mains left on.'

It is dangerous to treat the Scriptures as if they were only the words of a man. We are holding the very Word of God in our hands!

How do you read your Bible? Like a shopper in a super-market, only picking the verses that suit you? As if it were a newspaper article, only reflecting an individual's opinion? As if you were connected to the main power supply? Reflect on the fact that you are holding the very Word of God in your hands. Do you need to make changes to how you read the Bible? Ask God to show you Christ through the Scriptures. Pray that God would show you how inspired and powerful his Word is. Prepare to be amazed!

Day 25

Read 2 Timothy 3:1–17
Key verses: 2 Timothy 3:16–17

....

[16]All Scripture is God-breathed and is useful for teaching, rebuking, correcting and training in righteousness, [17]so that the servant of God may be thoroughly equipped for every good work.

Sometimes when pressures mount and the constant plate-spinning wears us down, we skip our Bible reading so that we can get on with our 'to-do' list. It seems such a luxury to read the Bible when so much else needs our attention. But, in fact, the opposite is true. It's in studying and meditating on God's Word that we're equipped to handle all that God allows into our lives.

Today, look again at verses 16–17. Paul wants us to grasp this fundamental truth: because the Scriptures are God-breathed, they are the means of completely equipping each Christian.

He explains that the Bible is useful for *teaching*. We need to study the Bible individually and in small groups; we need to hear expository preaching; the Bible must become our authority so that we learn how to please God in all things. At times, God's Word will be uncomfortable to read because it is useful for *rebuking*. The Scriptures show us what is wrong; they expose the darkness that needs to be brought to light. The Bible is also useful for *correcting* (*epanorthosis*). This word means 'lifting a person back on his or her feet', restoring them to a true way of living.

Paul goes on to say that the Scriptures are necessary for *training in righteousness*. This means to be made like Christ, conforming to his will and his way in every aspect of life. 'That the servant of God' – the minister, preacher, leader, but also any Christian – 'may be thoroughly equipped'. It is only as we grow in the Scriptures, obeying, learning and responding, that we can truly be complete and thoroughly equipped for the ministry of Christ.

The Bible is God's gift to us. Jesus never took up a pen, but the Holy Spirit was entrusted with bringing the truth to the apostles and, through them, to you and me.

We often fall into the trap of thinking that reading the Bible is a duty rather than a delight. Yes, we will have days when we seem to be going through the motions. But even on those days, God is using his Word to cleanse, refine and equip us. The Bible is God's gift to us to help us navigate our way through life, to deal with uncertainties, face hardships, cope with the demands of ministry and service. Don't cut yourself off from God's voice. Ask him to graciously use his Word to teach, rebuke, correct and train you in righteousness so that you are thoroughly equipped for all that he puts in your path – today and every day.

Day 26

Read 2 Timothy 4:1–22
Key verses: 2 Timothy 4:1–4

....

> [1] In the presence of God and of Christ Jesus, who will judge the living and the dead, and in view of his appearing and his kingdom, I give you this charge: [2] preach the word; be prepared in season and out of season; correct, rebuke and encourage – with great patience and careful instruction. [3] For the time will come when people will not put up with sound doctrine. Instead, to suit their own desires, they will gather round them a great number of teachers to say what their itching ears want to hear. [4] They will turn their ears away from the truth and turn aside to myths.

An individual's last words are significant because they tell us what that person's priorities and passions were. Chapter 4 is Paul's last will and testament to Timothy. And, not surprisingly, his major concern is the gospel.

He charges Timothy to 'Preach the word'. Timothy has been commanded to follow it, guard it, learn it, teach it to others, and now to preach it. To the world, preaching is folly. Many won't endure sound teaching. They want something new to tickle their ears and are easily led away from the truth and into myths. But, despite this opposition, all who love Christ and believe his Word need to teach and preach it.

'Be prepared in season and out of season.' Be willing to speak God's truth both when it is welcomed and when it's not. Don't desert your post even if the going gets tough.

However, readiness to speak is not an invitation to be arrogant or rude. Paul's charge to Timothy is to 'correct, rebuke and encourage – with great patience and careful instruction'. We need to be able to explain the gospel without being argumentative and loud, allowing God's Word to bring its own comfort and discomfort to people. We need to appeal for conversion and consecration, and steadily to expound God's Word with patience.

Why persevere? Why keep patiently explaining the gospel amidst such opposition? Well, Paul gives his charge to Timothy in 'the presence of God and Christ Jesus'. Ultimately we are all answerable, not to man, but to Christ, 'who will judge the living and the dead'. One day we will face Jesus as our Judge, Lord and King. On that day we shall hand back to him our ministries and all that he has entrusted to us.

What are your main priorities in life? Not all of us are preachers, but sharing the gospel should still be a high priority for us. Think about the ministry that God has given you. What opportunities are there to share the gospel? As you serve God today, remember that you are doing it in 'the presence of God and Christ Jesus'. Imagine the day when you will hand back to God all the fruits of your service. Keep that scene of heaven in your mind as you serve him joyfully, patiently and with great endurance.

Day 27

Read 2 Timothy 4:1–22
Key verse: 2 Timothy 4:5

....

[5] But you, keep your head in all situations, endure hardship, do the work of an evangelist, discharge all the duties of your ministry.

It's common for business, charities and even churches to draw up a mission statement. This is a document outlining their core purposes and objectives, which remain unchanged throughout the years. Verse 5 is the mission statement that Paul wants us and his young friend Timothy to live by.

Paul is in his prison cell, in chains, about to be martyred for the gospel, and he has poured out his soul in this letter to Timothy. Now, he sums up his message to Timothy and to the whole church of God – past, present and future – in this four-point charter.

1. *Keep your head in all situations.* Don't lose your nerve. Don't be blown away by every new fad. Rather, hold on to the core truths of the faith. Keep Christ at the centre of your life and ministry.

2. *Endure hardship.* The great theme of 2 Timothy 1 – 2 is that suffering is inevitable for the servant of God. Like Timothy, when we are afraid, we need to remember that God has given us a spirit of love, power and self-discipline. Are you prepared to endure suffering?

3. *Do the work of an evangelist.* We aren't all given the spiritual gift of evangelism, but each one of us is charged to do the work of an evangelist. We need to be prepared, ready to take every opportunity to share our faith. This is the main task of every Christian and every church. The gospel is our primary focus.

4. *Discharge all the duties of your ministry.* Whatever task God has given you, see it through to the end. God has entrusted this task to you and he has equipped you for it. Please him by remaining faithful to your calling until the very end. Don't lose your steam in later years!

Often at New Year we set ourselves targets for the coming months – usually losing weight! But we don't often spend time thinking about our goals for life.

However, we all have them, and, consciously or unconsciously, they shape our values, behaviour and priorities. Be honest with yourself and ask: what are your core objectives, the goals you think are important and want to achieve? How does your mission statement compare to Paul's? What about adopting Paul's mission statement as your own? Memorize his key principles, repeat them often, and pray for God's help in applying them to every situation.

Day 28

Read 2 Timothy 4:1–22
Key verses: 2 Timothy 4:6–8

. . . .

⁶For I am already being poured out like a drink offering, and the time for my departure is near. ⁷I have fought the good fight, I have finished the race, I have kept the faith. ⁸Now there is in store for me the crown of righteousness, which the Lord, the righteous Judge, will award to me on that day – and not only to me, but also to all who have longed for his appearing.

We don't often spend time thinking about our own mortality, and yet it is the one certainty of life. Paul's farewell to Timothy is a challenge to us, regardless of the inevitable distractions, temptations and disappointments, to press on and to finish life's race well.

Paul sees himself as a sacrifice, a drink offering to his Lord. 'The time of my departure is near' – the word used is *analusis*, 'setting free'. It's the word used when a boat leaves harbour. For Paul, this is not a reluctant, but a purposeful departure. He's packed, ready to go, looking forward to all that lies ahead.

The three pictures in verse 7 are from chapter 2. The retiring soldier – 'I have fought the good fight.' The retiring athlete – 'I have finished the race.' The retiring farmer – 'I have kept the faith', which literally means 'gone on', like a farmer fulfilling a farming task.

All that Paul had encouraged Timothy to do is demonstrated in his own life. Like Christ, Paul has run the race set before him. He has endured suffering and despised the shame. His legs were in chains as this letter was being written. Now the joy was set before him, and Paul was looking forward to hearing the righteous Judge say, 'Well done' to his righteous servant.

So often, we resist pouring ourselves out to God as an offering; we'd rather live for our own goals and dreams. We're not ready to depart for heaven; it seems too much of a wrench to leave our loved ones and earthly treasures. We so easily lose sight of the fact that death is the greatest liberation, the start of a more real and precious life. We get caught up in preserving our lives when sacrifice is the only true way to live. Keep your eyes focused on eternity, to Christ's return and your heavenly reward. And pray that as you wait, you would persevere, able to say, 'I have fought the good fight, I have finished the race, I have kept the faith.'

Day 29

Read 2 Timothy 4:1–22
Key verses: 2 Timothy 4:9–21

....

⁹*Do your best to come to me quickly,* ¹⁰*for Demas, because he loved this world, has deserted me and has gone to Thessalonica. Crescens has gone to Galatia, and Titus to Dalmatia.* ¹¹*Only Luke is with me. Get Mark and bring him with you, because he is helpful to me in my ministry.* ¹²*I sent Tychicus to Ephesus.* ¹³*When you come, bring the cloak that I left with Carpus at Troas, and my scrolls, especially the parchments.*

¹⁴*Alexander the metalworker did me a great deal of harm. The Lord will repay him for what he has done.* ¹⁵*You too should be on your guard against him, because he strongly opposed our message.*

¹⁶*At my first defence, no one came to my support, but everyone deserted me. May it not be held against them.* ¹⁷*But the Lord stood at my side and gave me strength, so that through me the message*

*might be fully proclaimed and all the Gentiles might
hear it. And I was delivered from the lion's mouth.
[18] The Lord will rescue me from every evil attack and
will bring me safely to his heavenly kingdom. To him
be glory for ever and ever. Amen.*

*[19] Greet Priscilla and Aquila and the household of
Onesiphorus. [20] Erastus stayed in Corinth, and I left
Trophimus ill in Miletus. [21] Do your best to get here
before winter. Eubulus greets you, and so do Pudens,
Linus, Claudia and all the brothers and sisters.*

Church life is full of highs and lows. There are times of joy
and celebration when ministries are flourishing, people
come to Christ and others are being strengthened in their
faith. There are also times of sadness when the church
family suffers a bereavement or there is a harsh disagree-
ment between believers.

Paul experienced a full range of circumstances throughout his ministry. He'd been deserted by Demas who
'loved this world' and opposed by Alexander the metalworker. He'd known the joy of friends such as faithful
Luke and practical Mark. He'd had practical needs for
clothing and books. He had endured difficulties and times
of living simply. He'd received love and encouragement
from various Christian families. But he'd also experienced

the sadness of watching a friend face illness. And at the end of his life, in a lonely prison cell, he was eager to see the young pastor Timothy again.

The constant in these turbulent times was that 'the Lord stood at my side and gave me strength'. Like Paul, each of us can draw on the strength of Christ as we serve him. People will come and people will go, but God's resources are unlimited, inexhaustible and incomparable.

Pray through all the circumstances you will face today. Remember, the Lord is at your side, giving you strength. Entrust your loved ones to God's care and keeping. Often there is nothing we can do to alleviate the difficulties they face, but remember that the Lord is at their side. His resources are more than adequate for their deepest need. Pray that they would be aware of God's strength today.

Day 30

Read 2 Timothy 4:1–22
Key verse: 2 Timothy 4:22

....

22 The Lord be with your spirit. Grace be with you all.

How did Paul close his letter? With a formulaic 'God bless'? No. To Timothy specifically, he wrote in the singular, 'The Lord be with your spirit', and to the whole church reading this letter he added, 'Grace be with you all.'

This was Paul's final encouragement to Timothy. This whole letter was to urge him and us to live the one life that we have been given, totally committed to the Lord, prioritizing the core truths of the faith and the centrality of the gospel. This was Paul's own aim. Indeed, he saw himself not only chained in prison but, more importantly, chained to Christ, chained to the core truths of the faith and chained to the gospel. His main focus in this letter is to urge us to share his priorities and become better equipped, cleansed and trained for service. In this way, by God's mercy, at the end of our lives we might be able to say, 'I have fought the good fight, I have finished the race, I have kept the faith.'

In the light of this, to the church, Paul wrote, 'Grace be with you all.' Of course, the cross is the greatest demonstration of God's grace to us. He sent his Son to die in our place, to bring us salvation and forgiveness of sins. But daily we see evidence of God's grace overflowing in our lives. We can't earn this grace; it is totally unmerited. Our only response can be to give ourselves wholeheartedly to God's service.

As we do that, each of us can go into our day knowing that the Lord is with our spirit. We are not alone. We are not expected to serve God in our own strength. Our devotion to God is not a matter of simply trying harder. Whatever challenges, temptations and doubts we face, the ever-present, all-powerful God the Holy Spirit is with us, enabling and energizing our spirit. Yield yourself to his control, rely on his strength, submit to his authority and live daily for his pleasure.

What has God been saying to you through Paul's letter to Timothy? Pray through the truths that God wants you to cling on to, the priorities he wants you to invest your life in, the commands he wants you to follow and the promises he wants you to believe in. Know that 'the

Lord is with your spirit' – he will strengthen, comfort, guide and keep you. Learn to rely more and more on him, stay in step with him and keep your face turned to his, until the day he brings you home. Amen.

For further study

If you would like to do further study on 2 Timothy, the commentaries listed here may be useful.

- R. Kent Hughes, and Bryan Chapell, *1–2 Timothy and Titus: To Guard the Deposit*, Preaching the Word (Crossway, 2012).

- Walter L. Liefeld, *1 & 2 Timothy, Titus*, The NIV Application Commentary (Zondervan, 1999).

- John Stott, *The Message of 2 Timothy: Guard the Gospel*, The Bible Speaks Today (IVP, 1999).

- Charles R. Swindoll, *Insights on 1 & 2 Timothy, Titus*, Swindoll's Living Insights New Testament Commentary (Tyndale, 2014).

KESWICK MINISTRIES

Our purpose

Keswick Ministries is committed to the spiritual renewal of God's people for his mission in the world.

God's purpose is to bring his blessing to all the nations of the world. That promise of blessing, which touches every aspect of human life, is ultimately fulfilled through the life, death, resurrection, ascension and future return of Christ. All of the people of God are called to participate in his missionary purposes, wherever he may place them. The central vision of *Keswick Ministries* is to see the people of God equipped, encouraged and refreshed to fulfil that calling, directed and guided by God's Word in the power of his Spirit, for the glory of his Son.

Our priorities

Keswick Ministries seeks to serve the local church through:

- *Hearing God's Word*: the Scriptures are the foundation for the church's life, growth and mission, and *Keswick Ministries* is committed to preach and teach God's Word in a way that is faithful to Scripture and relevant to Christians of all ages and backgrounds.

- *Becoming like God's Son*: from its earliest days the Keswick movement has encouraged Christians to live godly lives in the power of the Spirit, to grow in Christ-likeness and to live under his lordship in every area of life. This is God's will for his people in every culture and generation.

- *Serving God's mission*: the authentic response to God's Word is obedience to his mission, and the inevitable result of Christlikeness is sacrificial service. *Keswick Ministries* seeks to encourage committed discipleship in family life, work and society, and energetic engagement in the cause of world mission.

Our ministry

Keswick: the event. Every summer the town of Keswick hosts a three-week Convention, which attracts some 15,000 Christians from the UK and around the world. The event provides Bible teaching for all ages, vibrant worship, a sense of unity across generations and denominations, and an inspirational call to serve Christ in the world. It caters for children of all ages and has a strong youth and young adult programme. And it all takes place in the beautiful Lake District – a perfect setting for rest, recreation and refreshment.

- **Keswick: the movement**. For 140 years the work of Keswick has impacted churches worldwide, and today the movement is underway throughout the UK, as well as in many parts of Europe, Asia, North America, Australia, Africa and the Caribbean. *Keswick Ministries* is committed to strengthen the network in the UK and beyond, through prayer, news, pioneering and cooperative activity.

- **Keswick resources**. *Keswick Ministries* is producing a growing range of books and booklets based on the core foundations of Christian life and mission. It makes Bible teaching available through free access to mp3 downloads, and the sale of DVDs and CDs. It broadcasts online through Clayton TV and annual BBC Radio 4 services. In addition to the summer Convention, *Keswick Ministries* is hoping to develop other teaching and training events in the coming years.

Our unity

The Keswick movement worldwide has adopted a key Pauline statement to describe its gospel inclusivity: 'for you are all one in Christ Jesus' (Galatians 3:28). *Keswick Ministries* works with evangelicals from a wide variety of church backgrounds, on the understanding that they share a commitment to the essential truths of the Christian faith as set out in our statement of belief.

Our contact details
T: 01768 780075
E: info@keswickministries.org
W: www.keswickministries.org
Mail: Keswick Ministries, Convention Centre,
Skiddaw Street, Keswick CA12 4BY, England

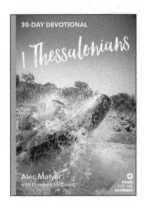

related titles from IVP

FROM THE FOOD FOR THE JOURNEY SERIES

1 Thessalonians
Alec Motyer
with Elizabeth McQuoid

ISBN: 978-1-78359-439-9
112 pages, paperback

The Food for the Journey series takes messages by well-loved
Bible teachers at the Keswick Convention and reformats them into
accessible daily devotionals.

*'This helpful series will facilitate a prayerful, intelligent, systematic
reading of the Bible, so that God's voice is clearly heard. There is no
greater service than to promote a daily reading of the Word – God
will nourish, encourage, rebuke and correct us, all to his glory!'*
David Cook

*'A heart-warming, mind-stretching, spine-strengthening series –
essential daily nourishment from God's Word for disciples on the
move.'* Jonathan Lamb

*'This devotional series is biblically rich, theologically deep and full
of wisdom that will strengthen, nourish and guide you in learning
how to live life from God's perspective. I recommend it highly!'*
Becky Pippert

*'Highly accessible and peppered with thoughtful insights and
penetrating questions, these devotional guides are excellent tools to
enable us to hear God's Word in our day-to-day lives.'* John Risbridger

Related Teaching CD Packs

1 Thessalonians

Alec Motyer
SWP2203D

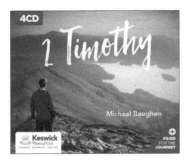

2 Timothy

Michael Baughen
SWP2202D

Available from **www.essentialchristian.com**

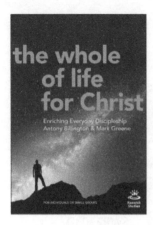

related titles from IVP

Discipleship Matters
Dying to live for Christ
Peter Maiden

ISBN: 978-1-78359-355-2
176 pages, paperback

Discipleship involves a gentle journey with our Saviour. Its demands will dovetail happily with our carefully crafted plans.

Wrong. Peter Maiden pulls no punches as he looks at what a disciple should look like today. Are we prepared to follow Jesus' example? Lose our lives for his sake? Live counter-culturally in a world that values power, prestige and money, and constantly puts self at the centre?

Of all people, Jesus, the Son of God, has the authority to require this of us. And he's calling us to a relationship, not to a set of rules or a miserable, spartan existence. In fact, it is through losing our lives that we find them, and thereby discover the source of pure joy.

What a pity we set the bar too low.

Available from your local Christian bookshop or **www.ivpbooks.com**

TIM CHESTER

MISSION MATTERS

Love Says Go

related titles from IVP

Mission Matters
Love says go
Tim Chester

ISBN: 978-1-78359-280-7
176 pages, paperback

The Father delights in his Son. This is the starting point of mission, its very core. The word 'mission' means 'sending'. But for many centuries this was only used to describe what God did, sending his Son and his Spirit into the world. World mission exists because the Father wants people to delight in his Son, and the Son wants people to delight in the Father.

Tim Chester introduces us to a cascade of love: love flowing from the Father to the Son through the Spirit. And that love overflows and, through us, keeps on flowing to our Christian community and beyond, to a needy world. Mission matters. This book is for ordinary individuals willing to step out and be part of the most amazing, exciting venture in the history of the world.

'If you want to fire up your church with a vision for global mission, this is your book! ... It should carry a spiritual health warning.'
David Coffey OBE

'I am sure this book will provoke many to respond to the challenge as they realize that there are still thousands waiting to be introduced to the Saviour.' Helen Roseveare

Available from your local Christian bookshop or **www.ivpbooks.com**

related titles

Knowing God Better

The Vision of the Keswick Movement
Jonathan Lamb

ISBN: 978-1-78359-369-9
112 pages, paperback

It's a remarkable story. It spans 140 years and crosses cultures and continents.

It has revolutionized hundreds of thousands of lives and it has had a radical impact on churches and communities. It has launched new mission movements and pushed forward the frontiers of the gospel. And it continues to grow, as Christians the world over see the urgent need for spiritual renewal.

Why has this happened? What are the marks of this spiritual movement? In *Knowing God Better*, Jonathan Lamb introduces the big priorities that shape the Keswick movement, priorities that are essential for the well-being of Christians and local churches around the world today.

'An inspiring reminder of biblical principles that should be in the heart of every disciple of Jesus Christ.' Elaine Duncan

'A heart-warming and soul-stirring introduction to a ministry and movement that seeks to bring glory to God by serving the church.' Liam Goligher

Available from your local Christian bookshop or **www.ivpbooks.com**